SUPER CUTE KIDS

Coloring Book

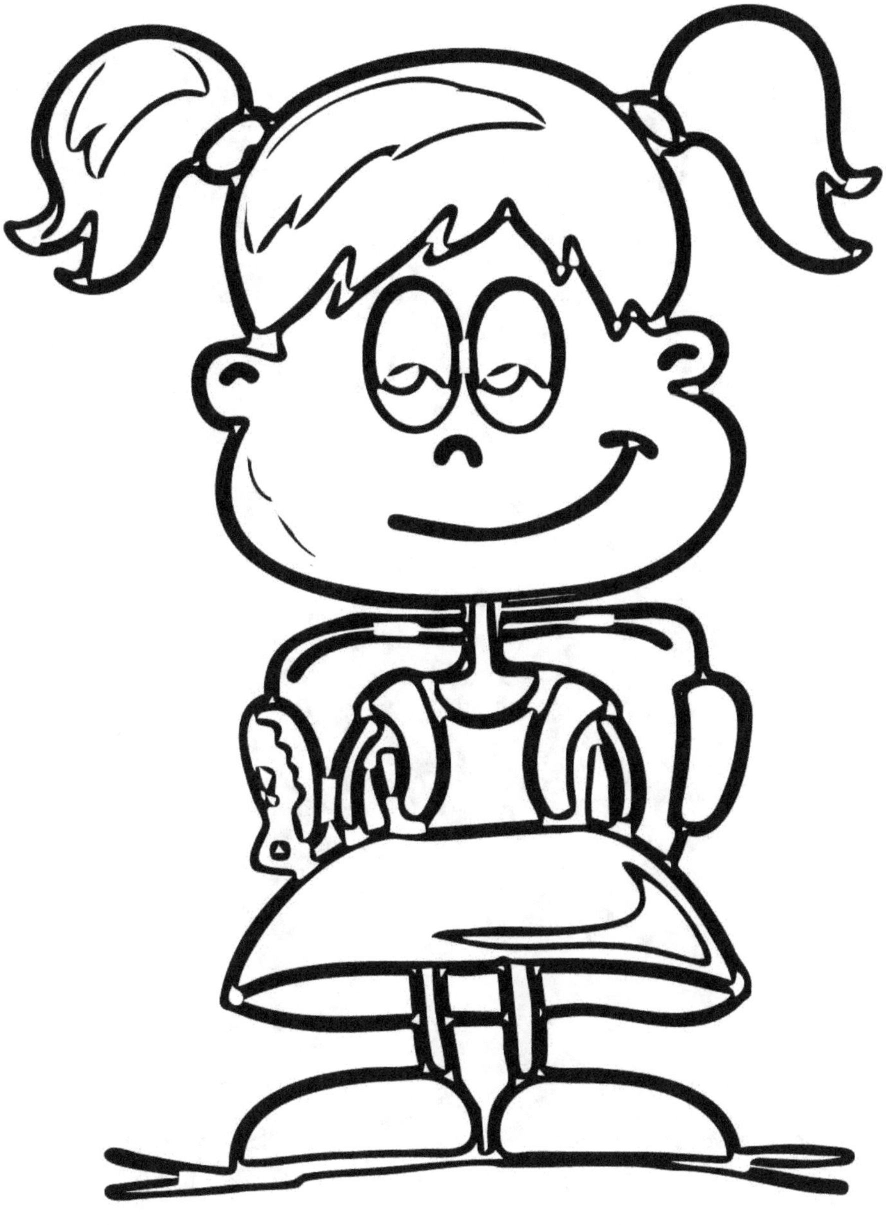

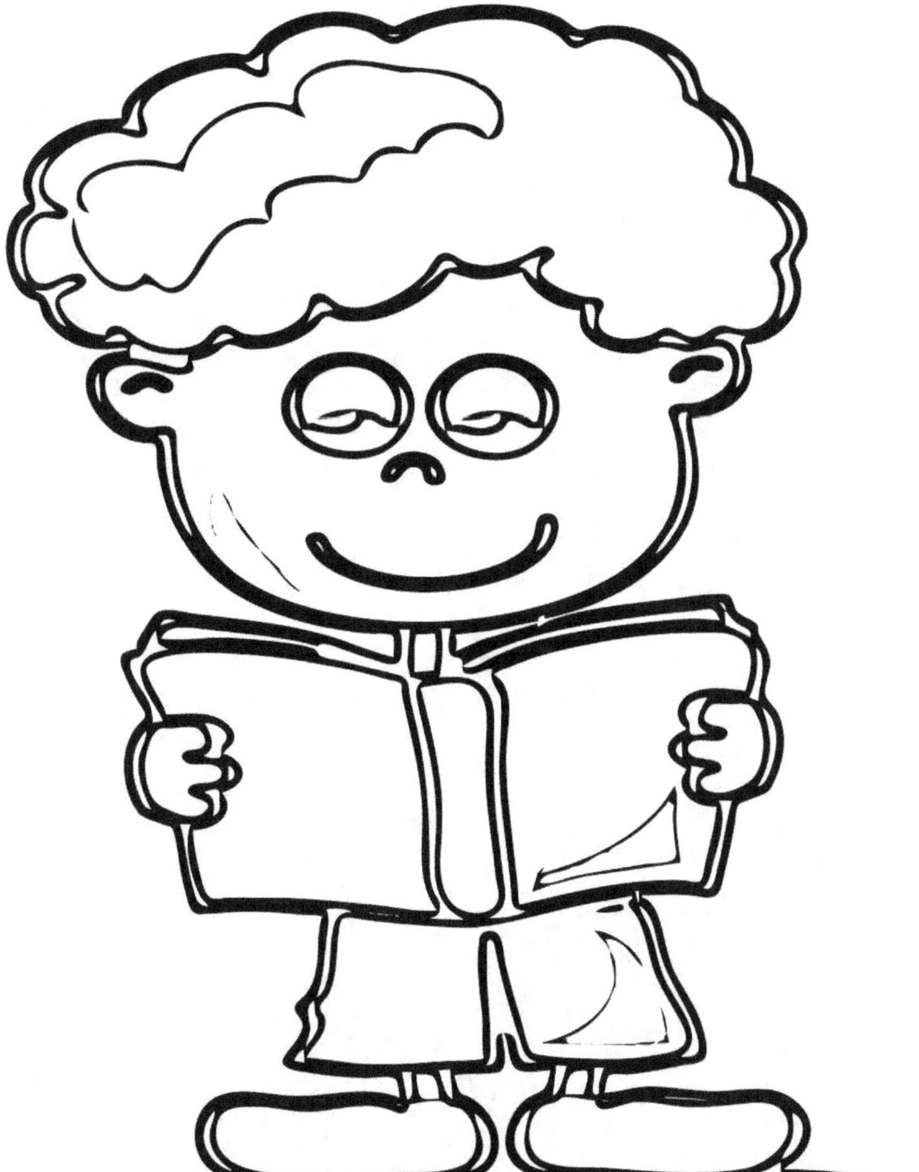

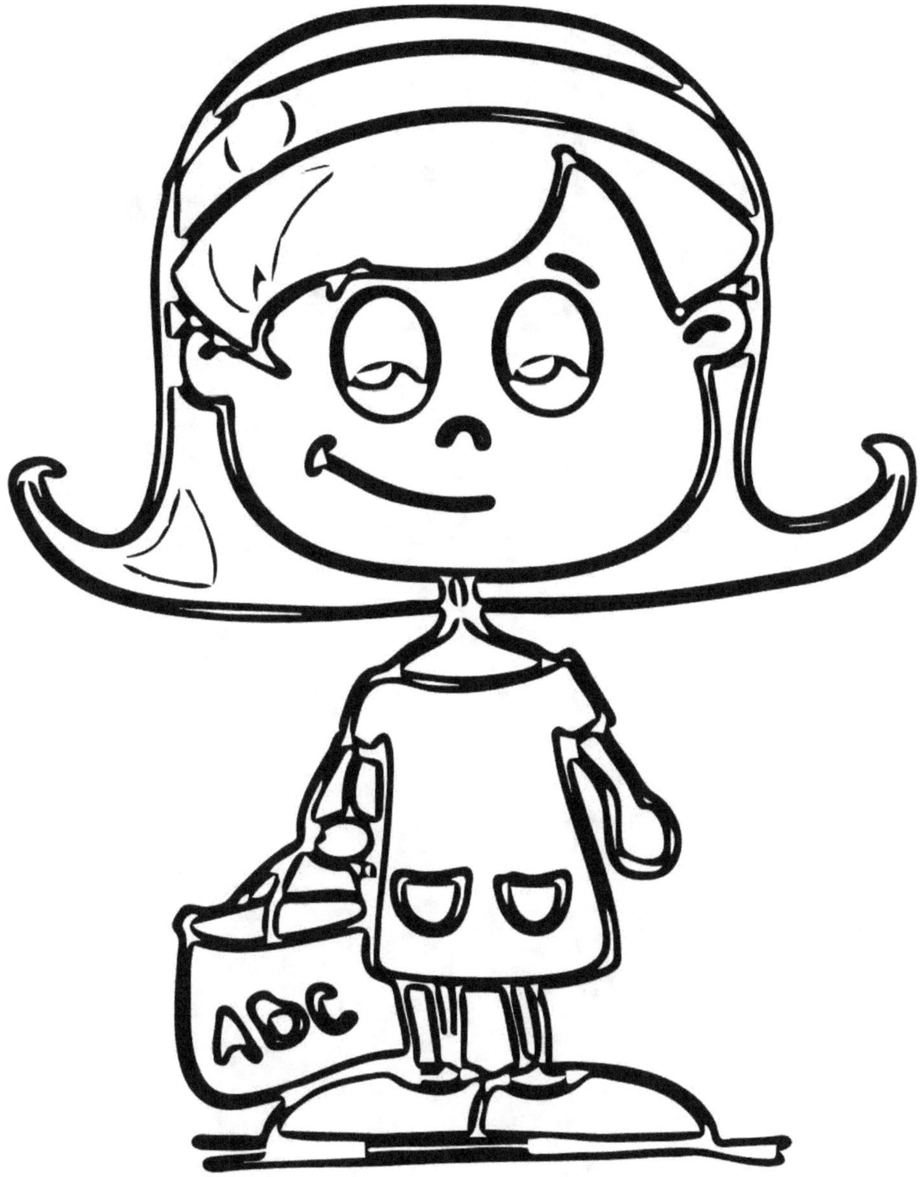
ABC

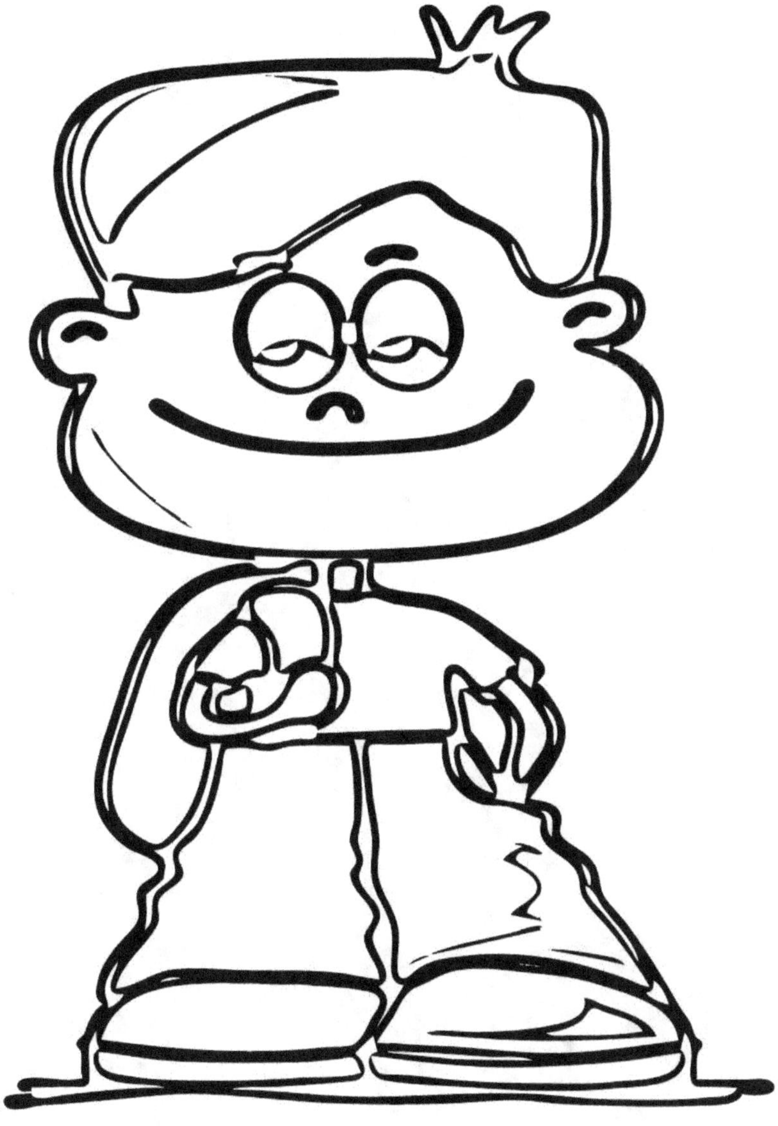

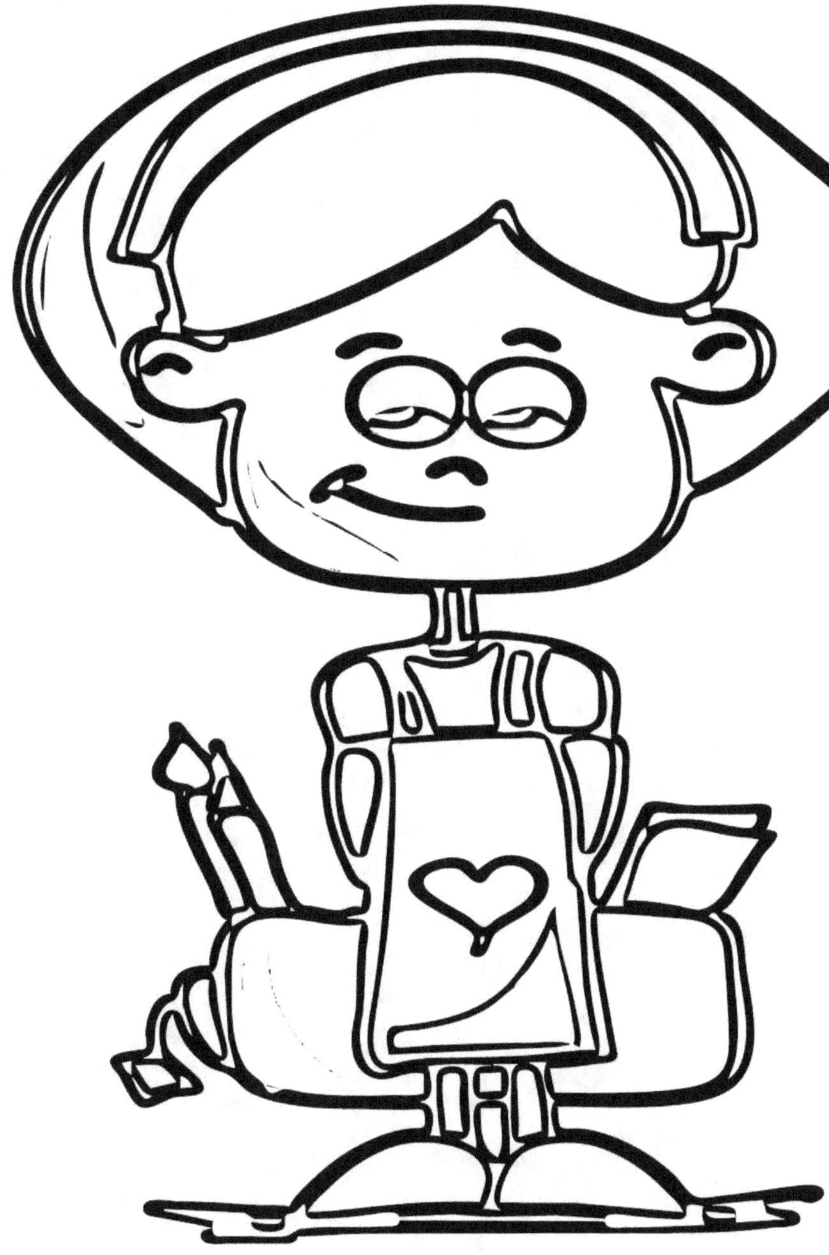

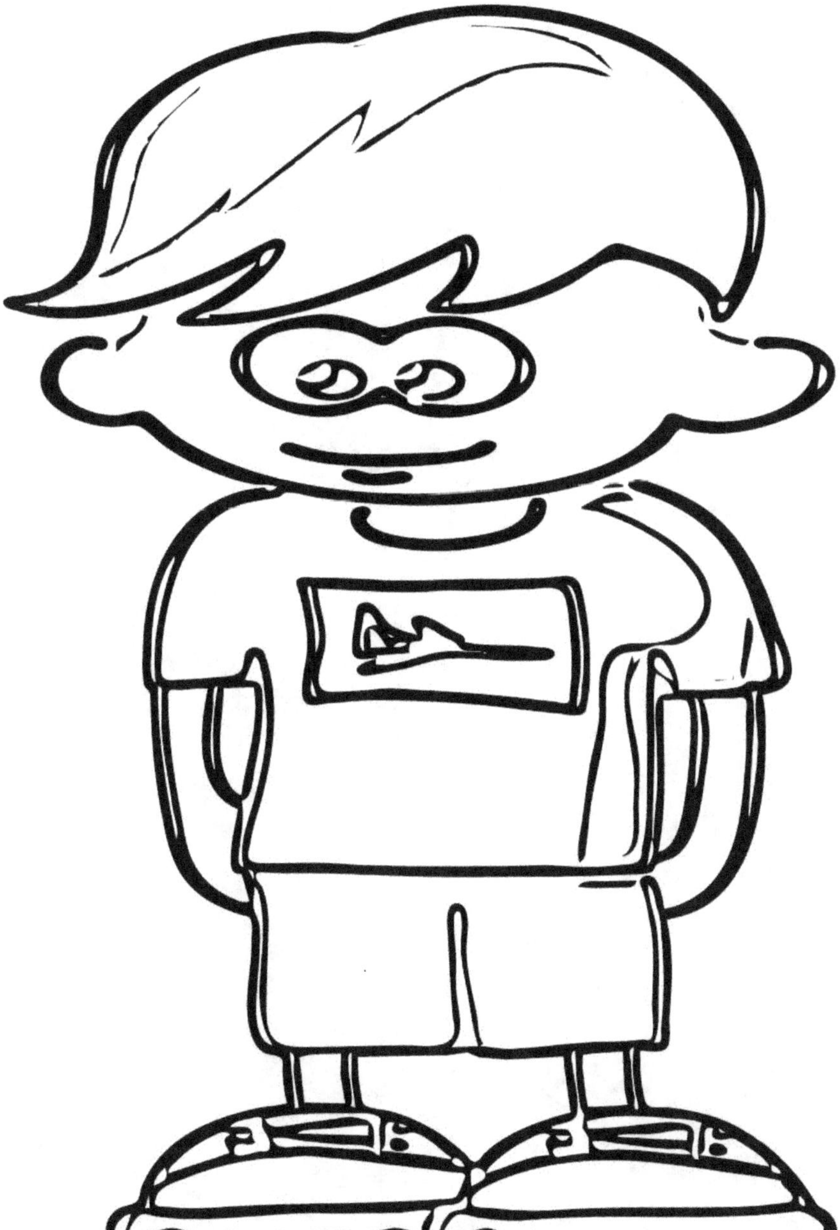

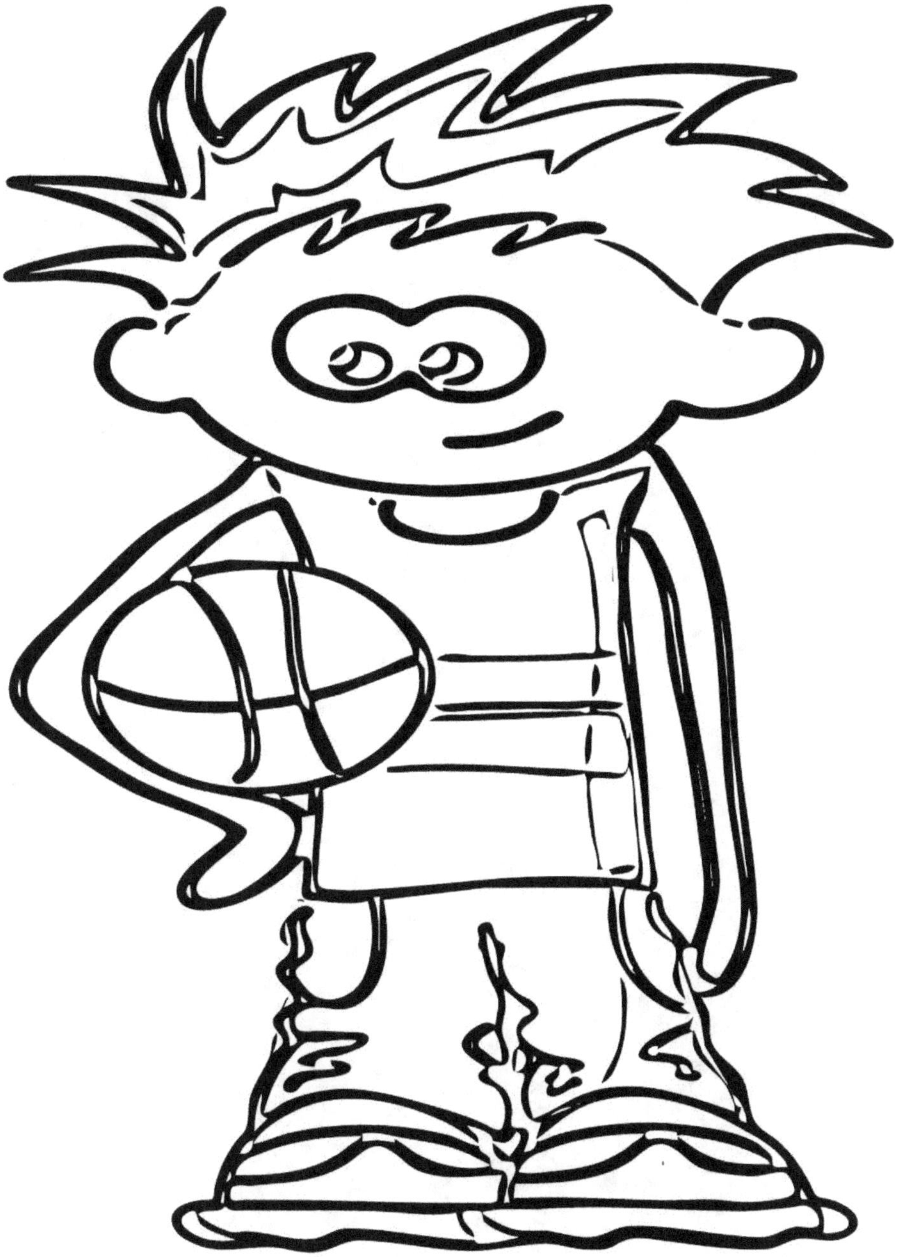

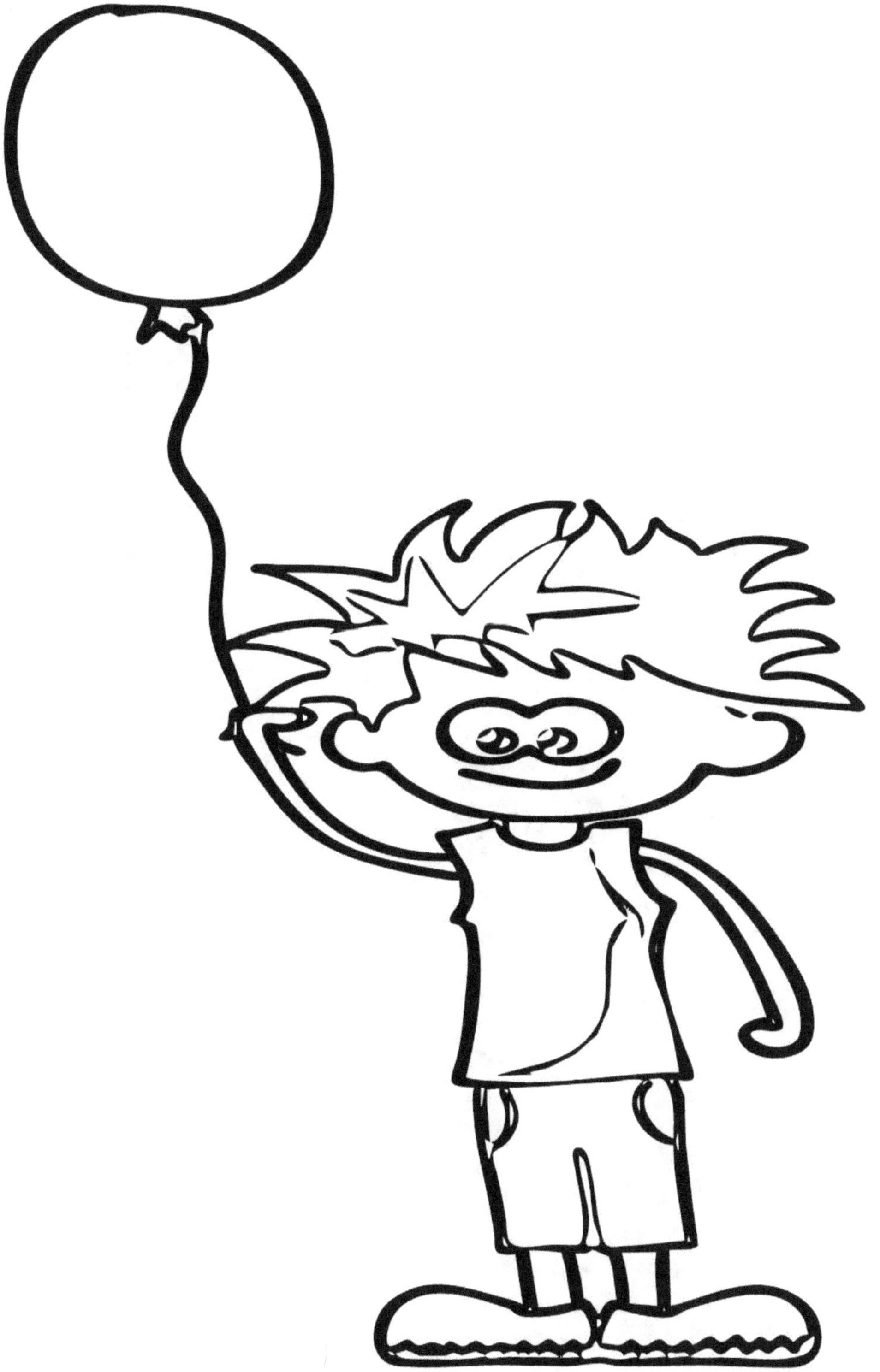

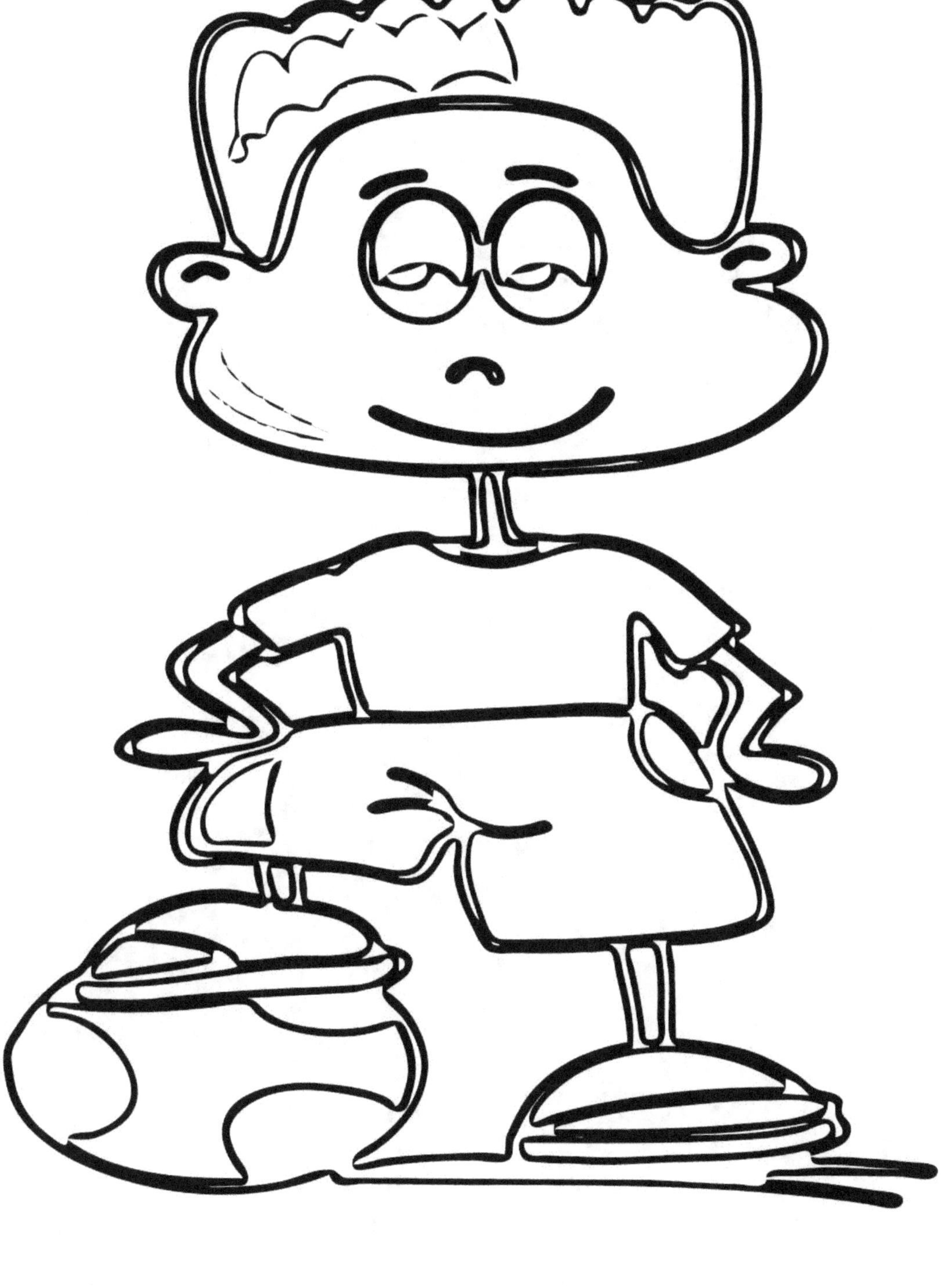

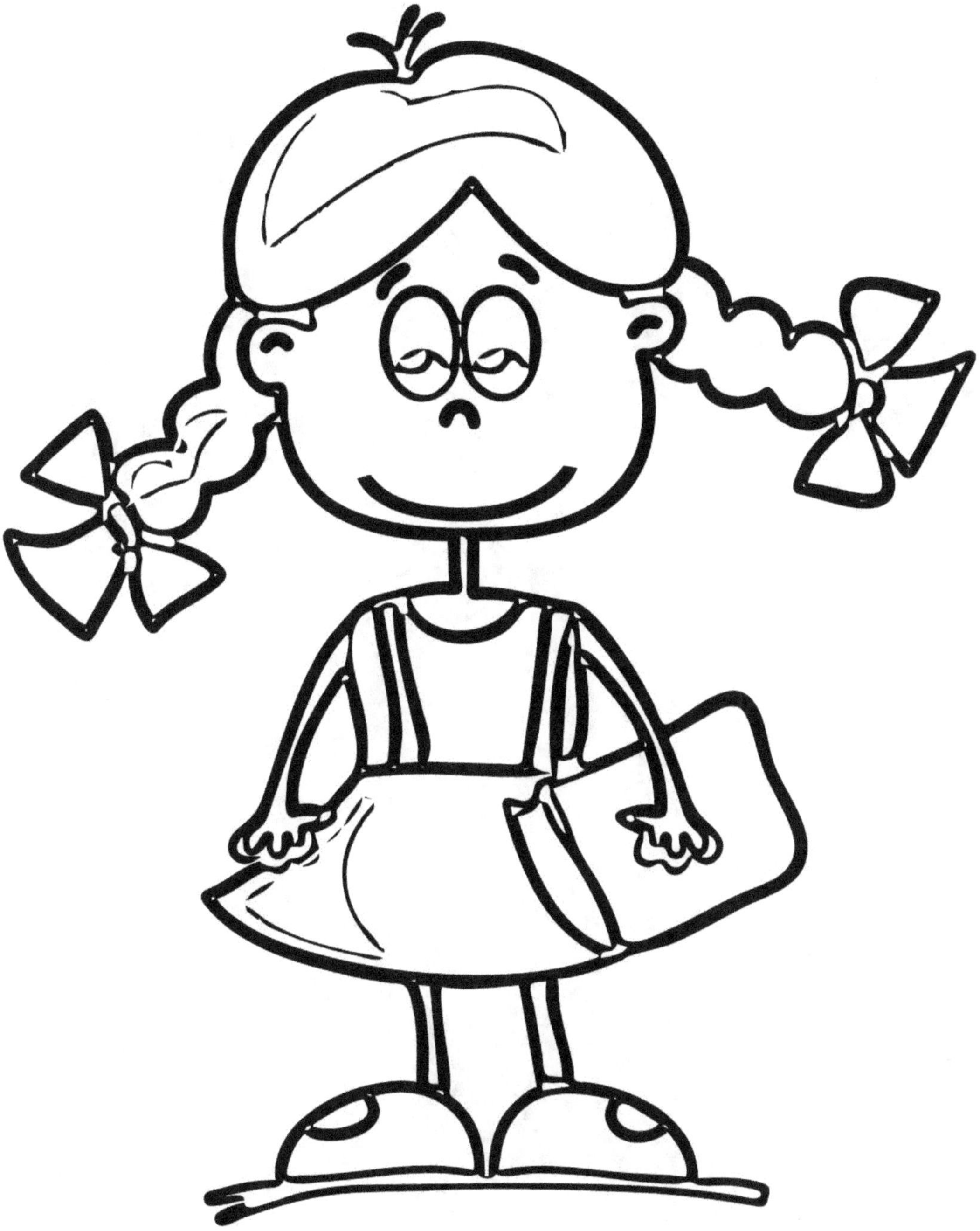

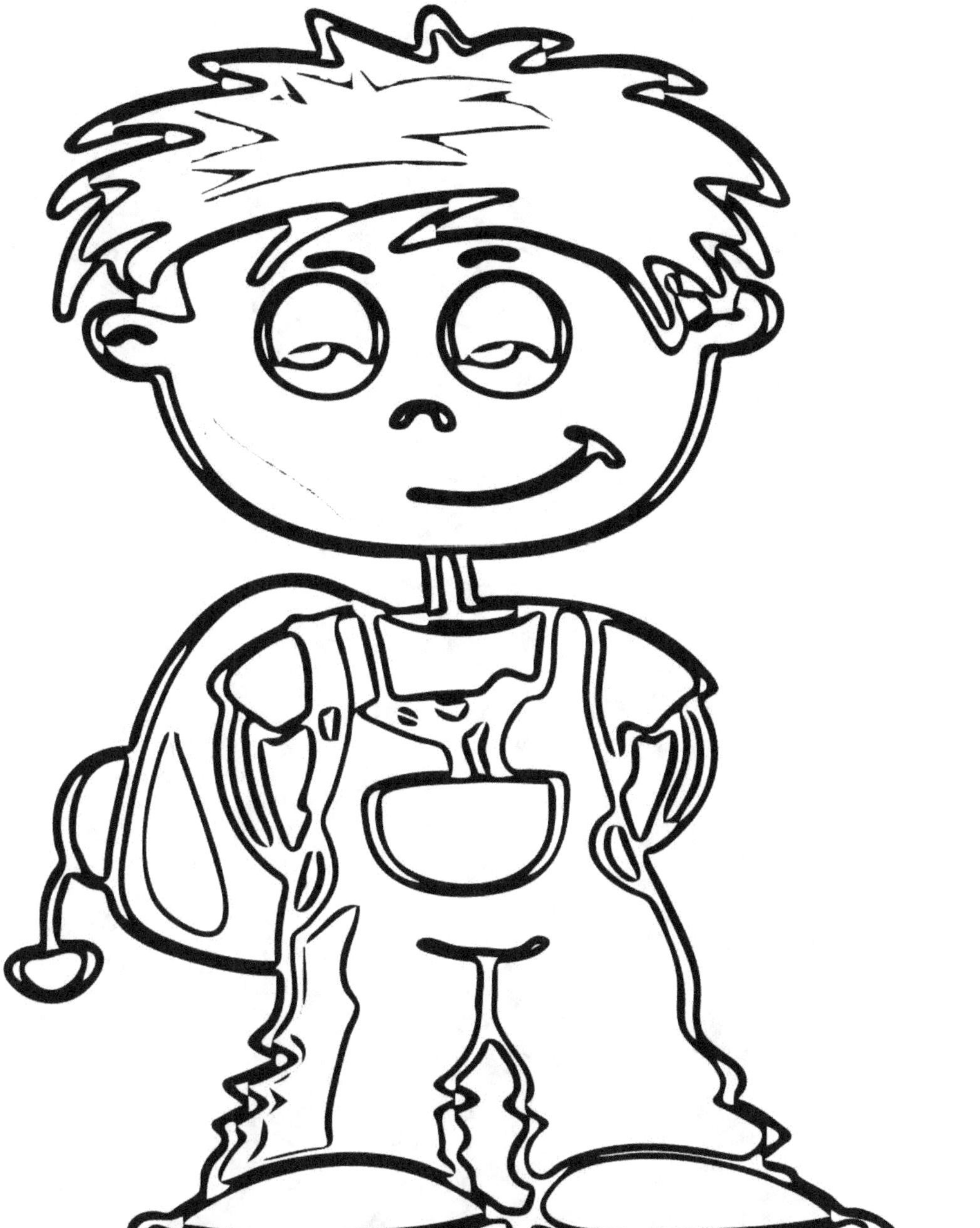

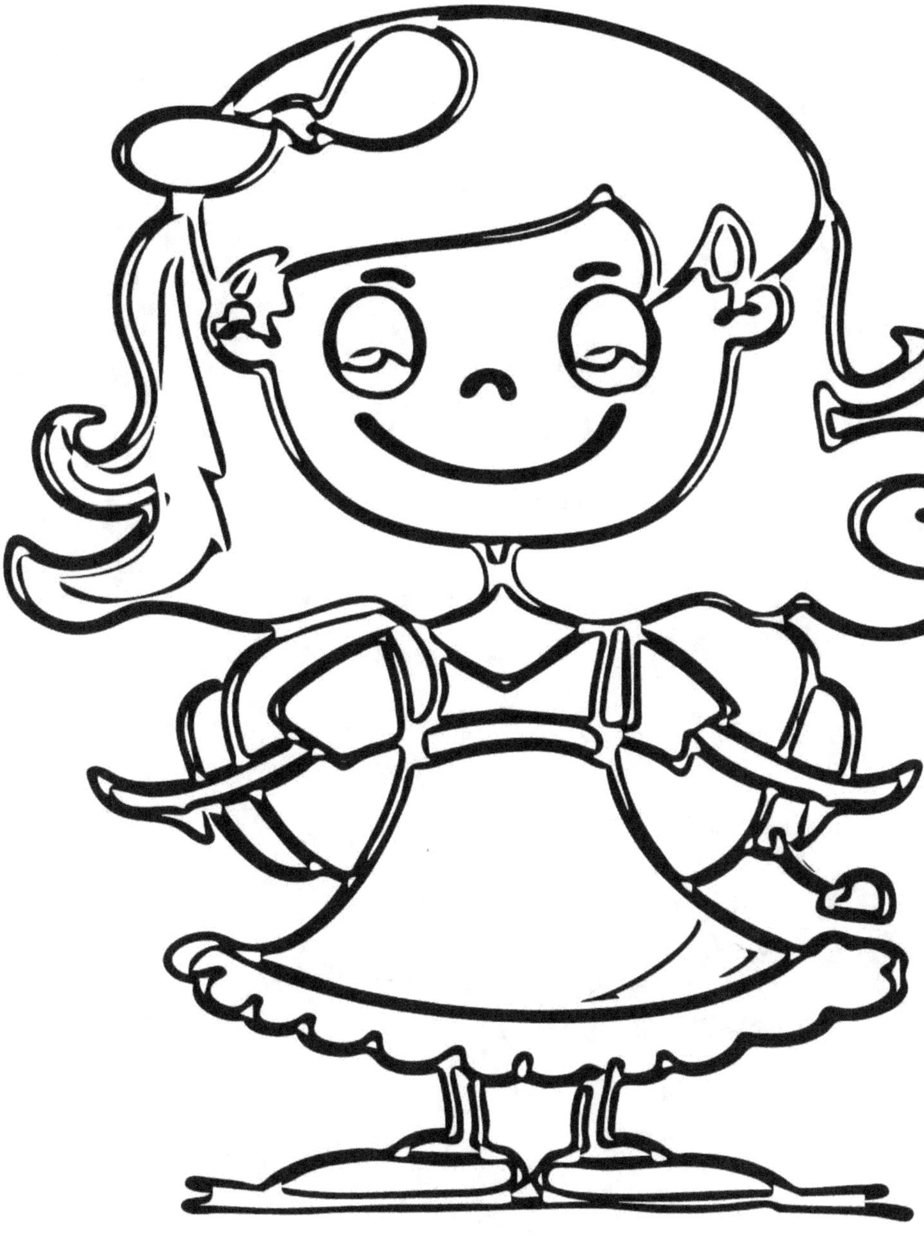

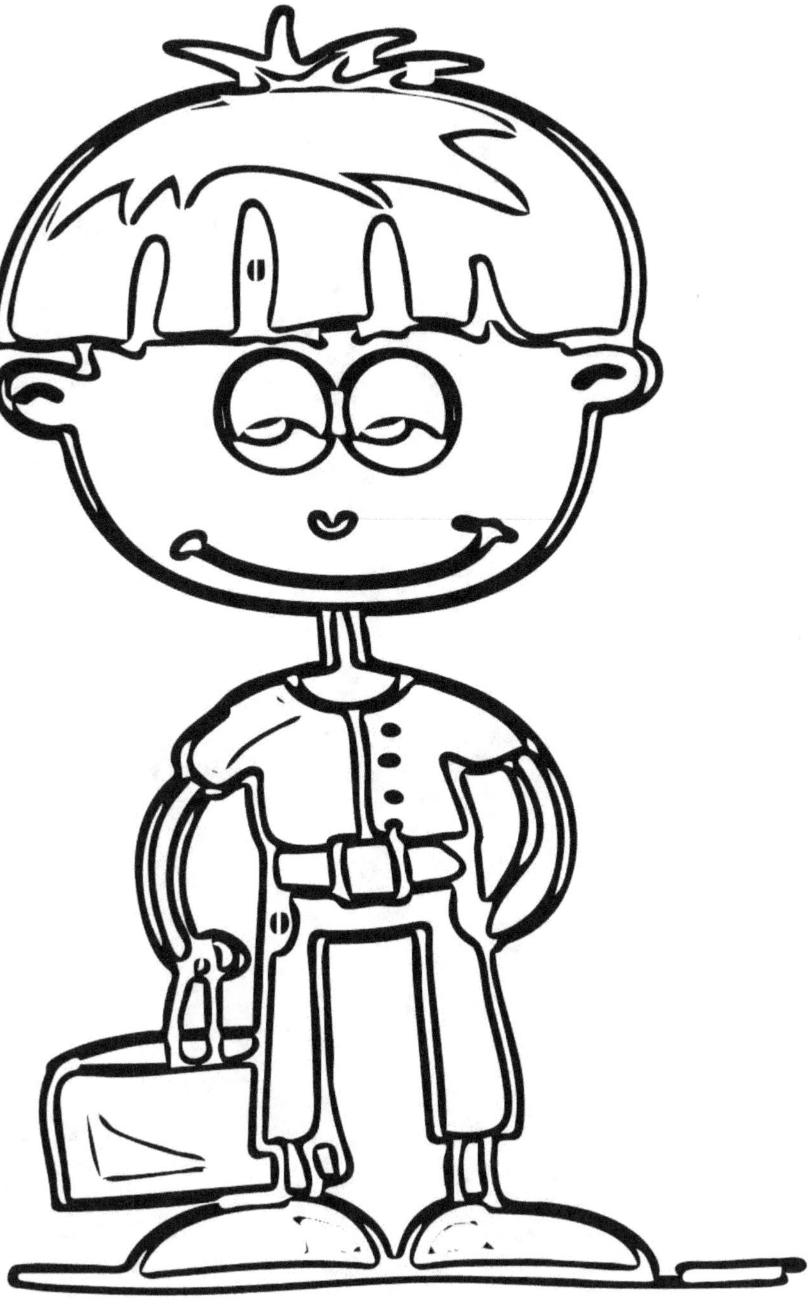

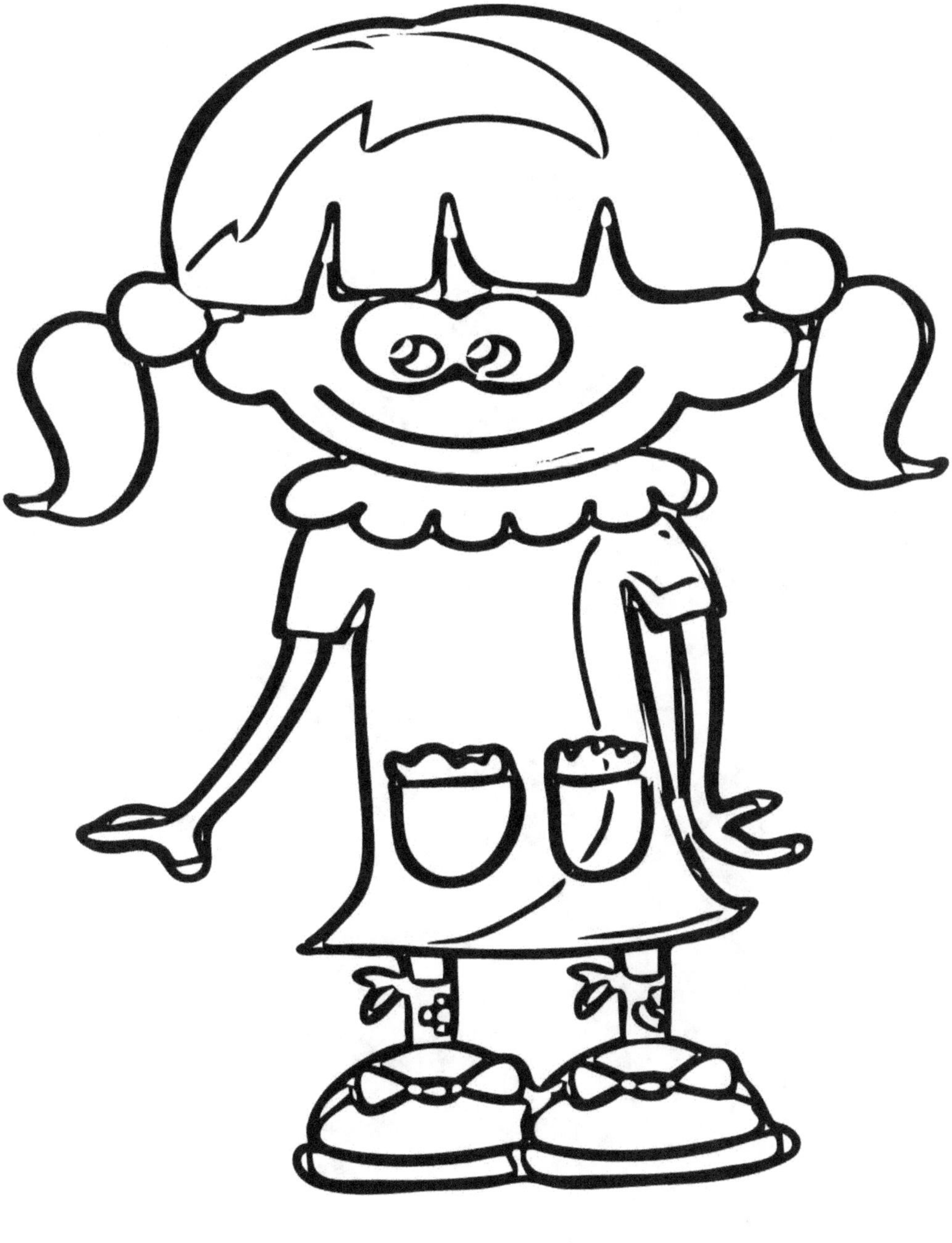

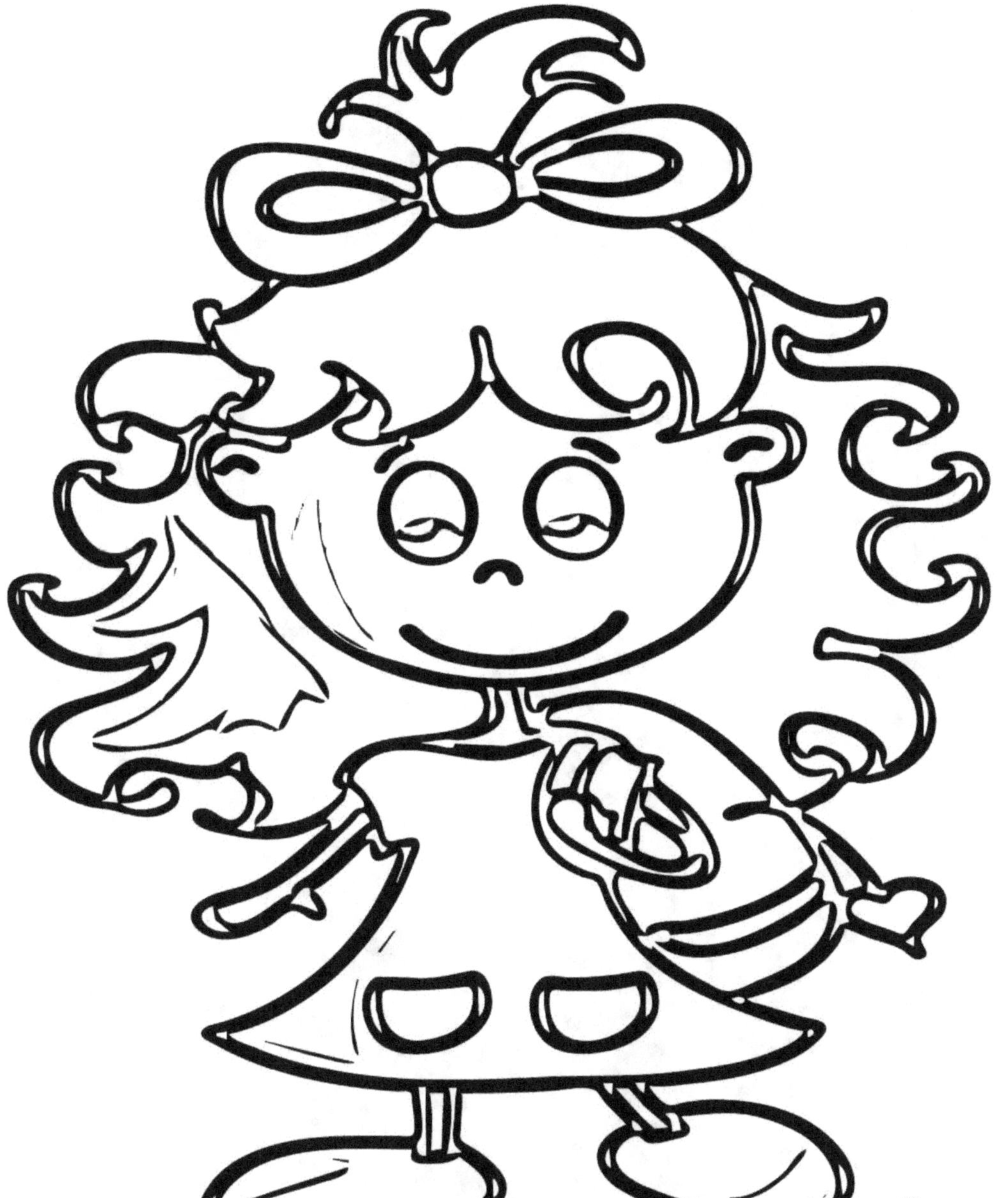

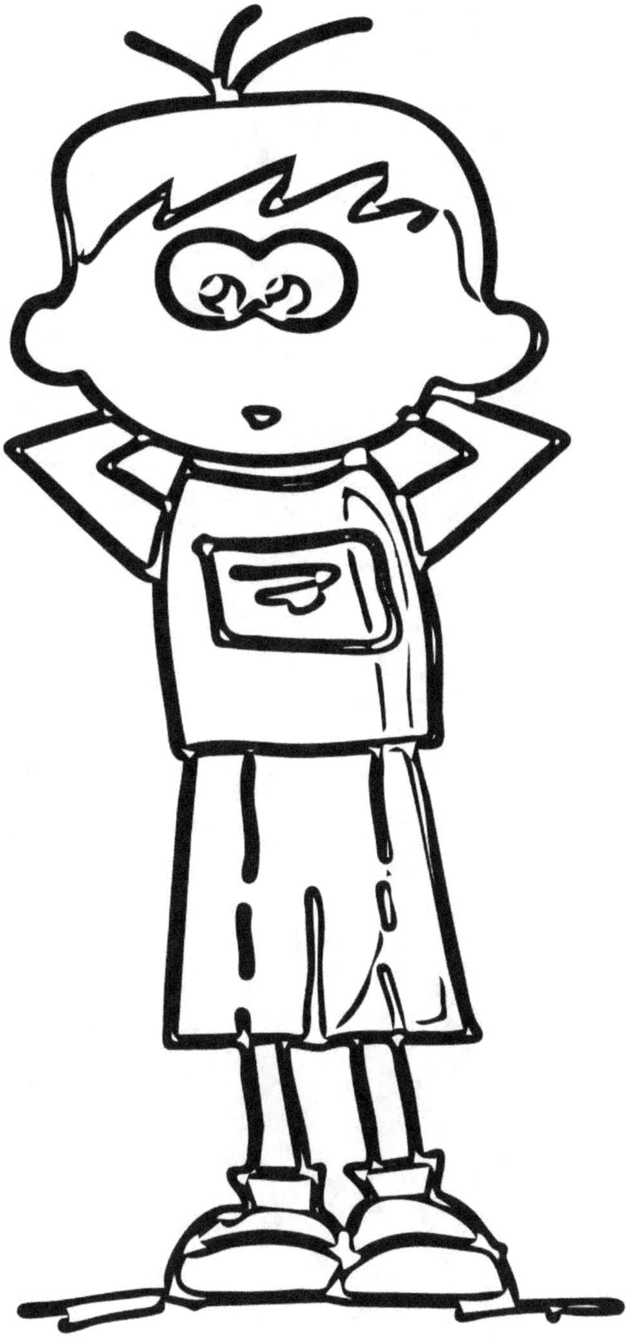

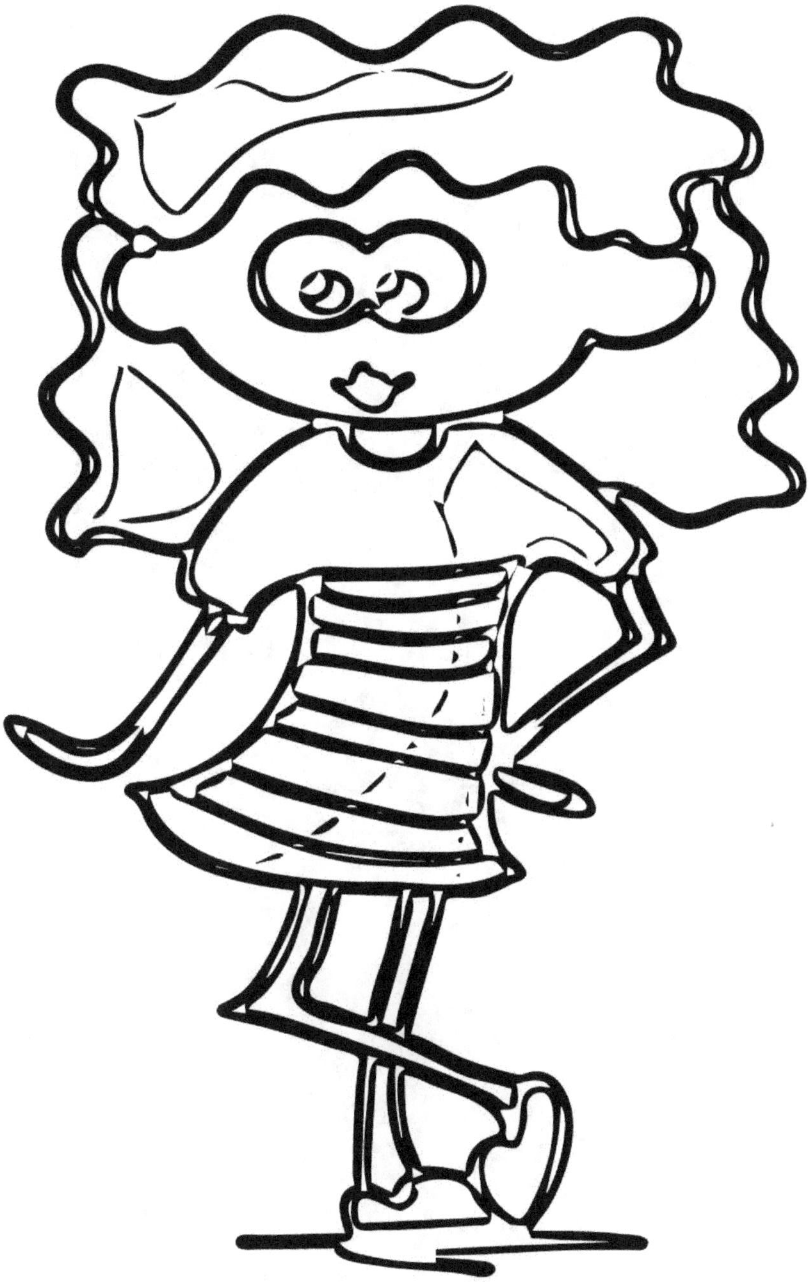

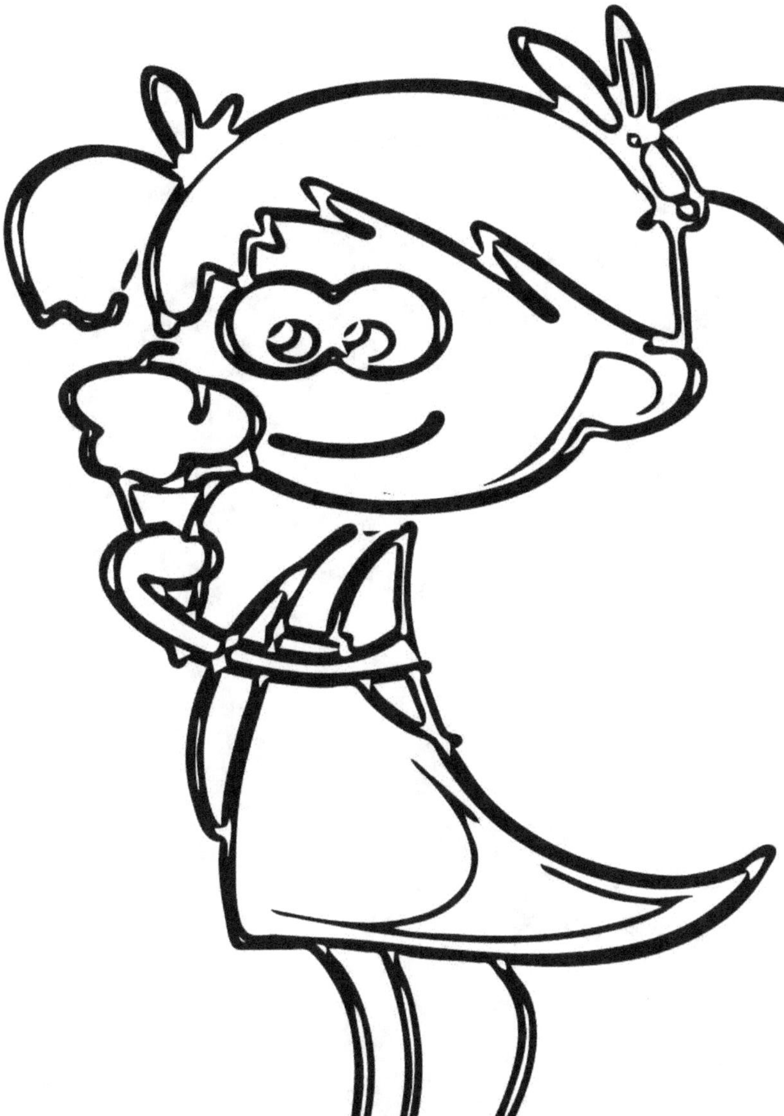

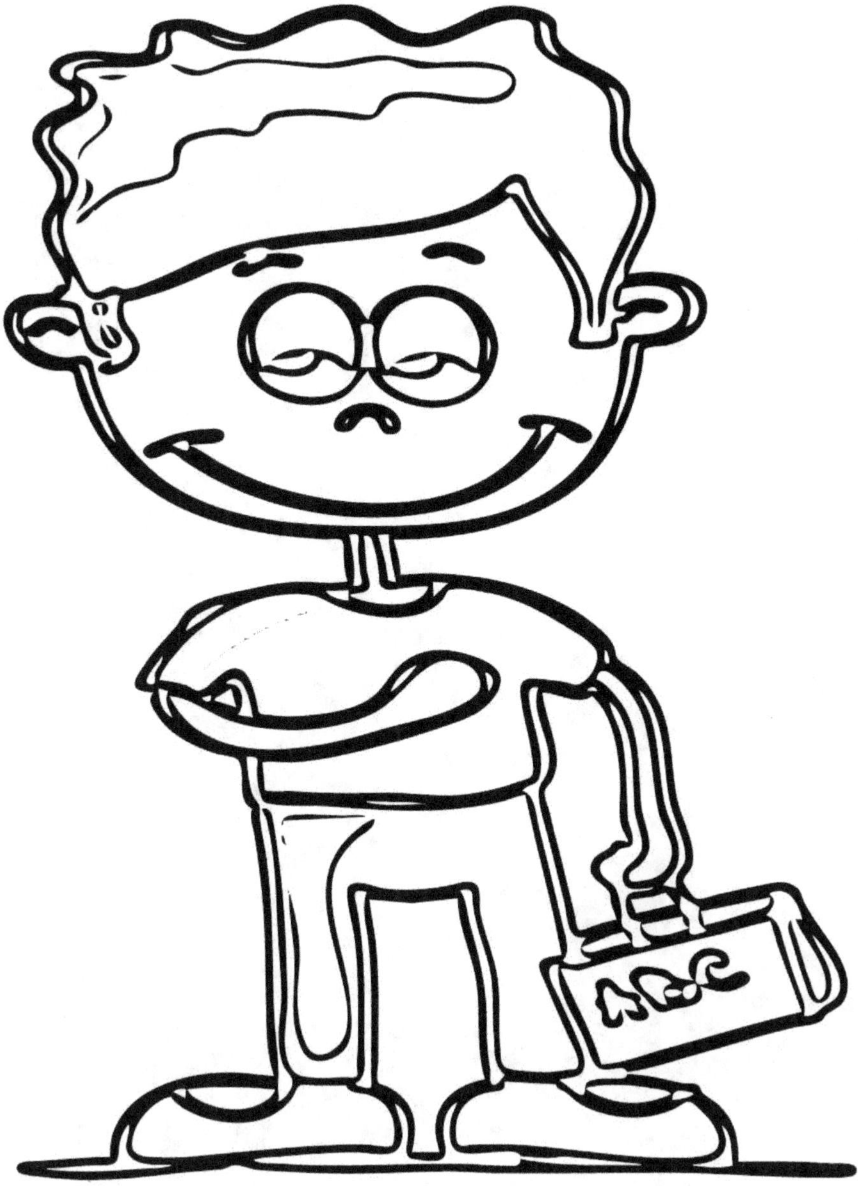
ABC

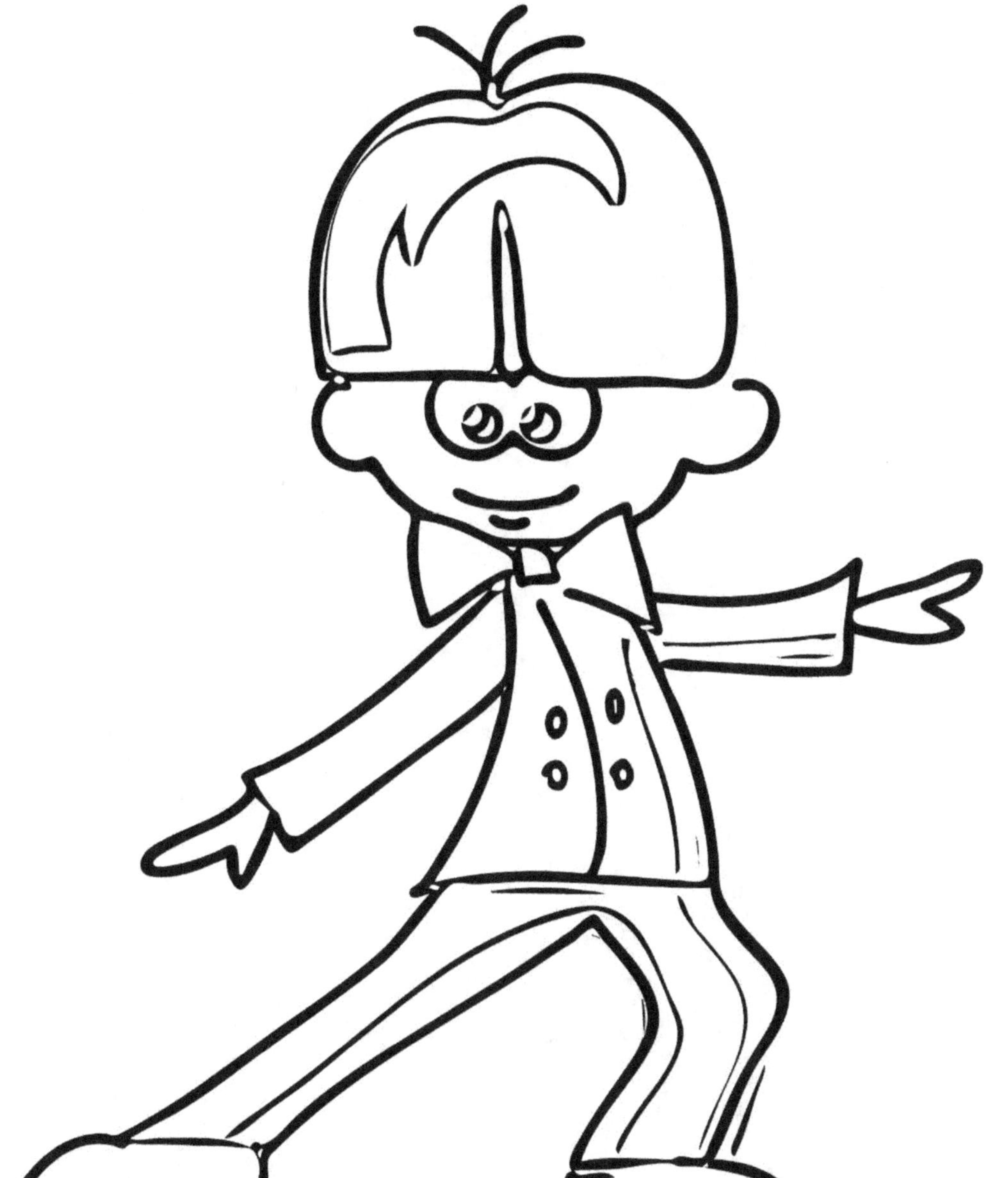

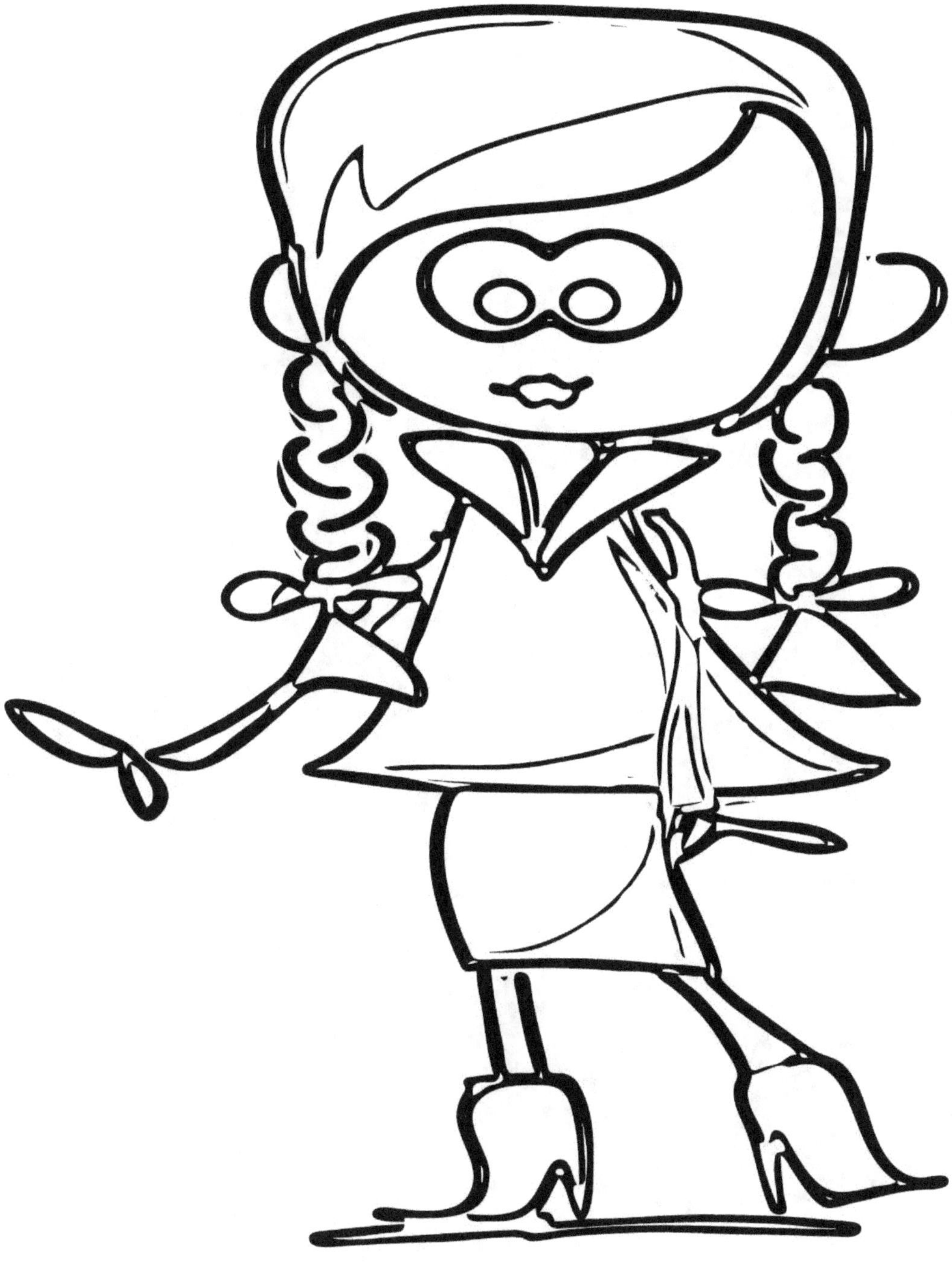

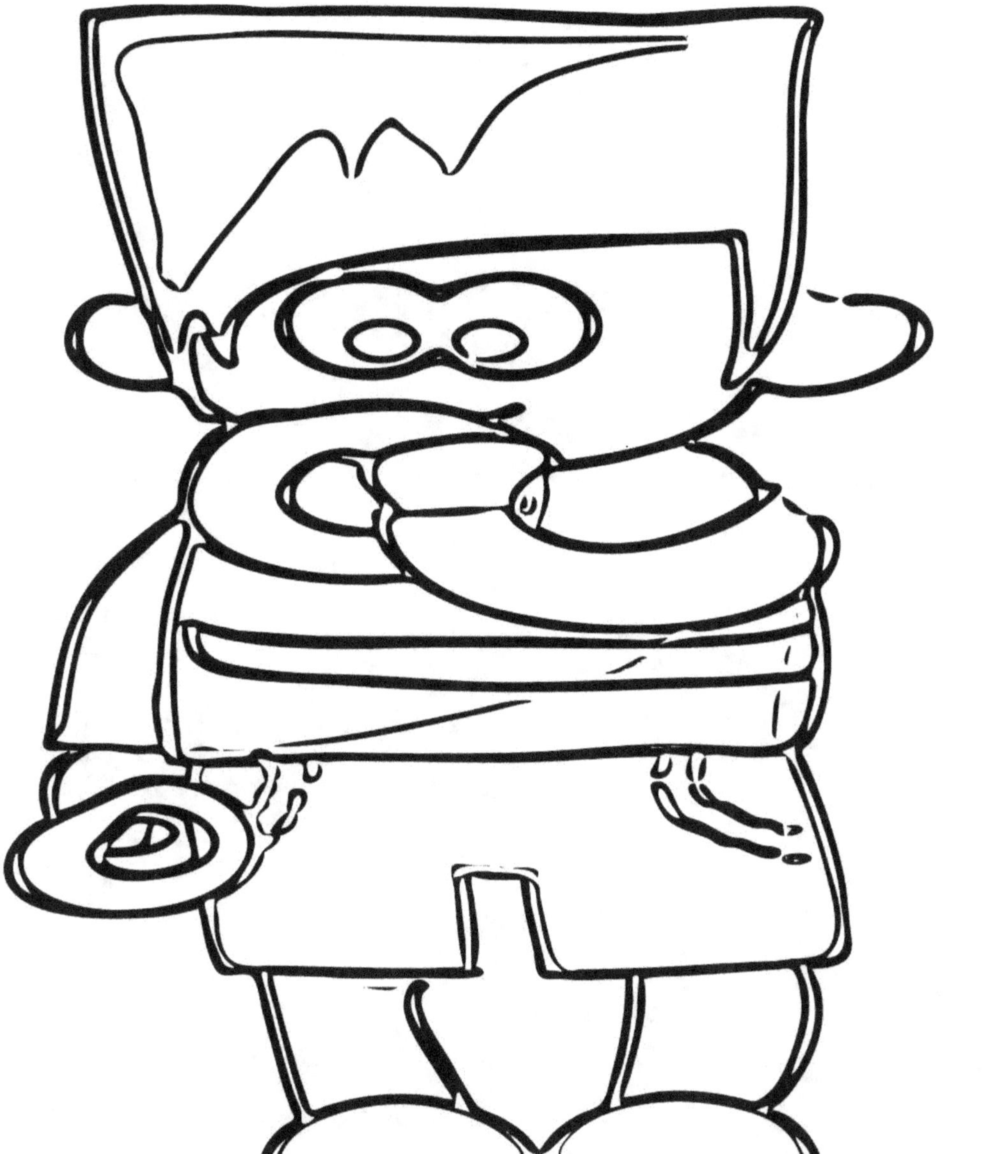

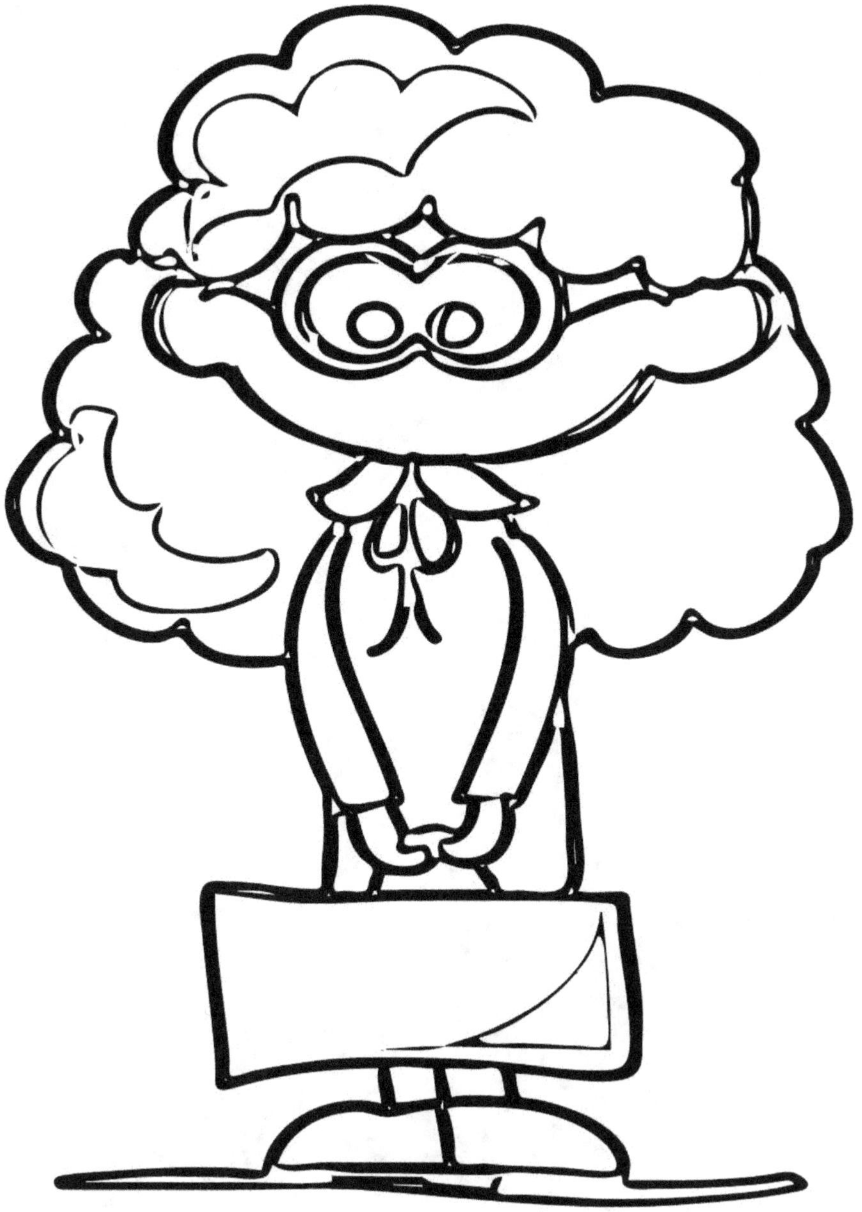

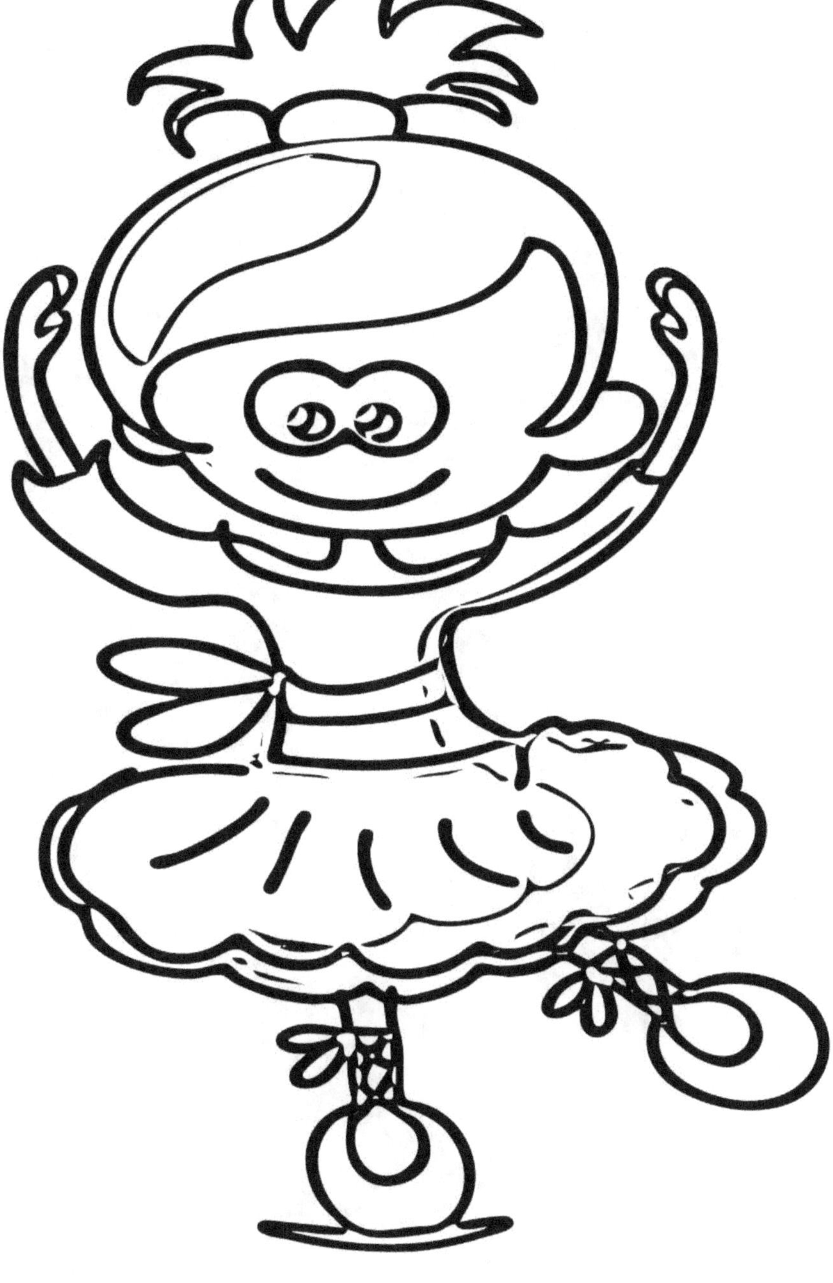

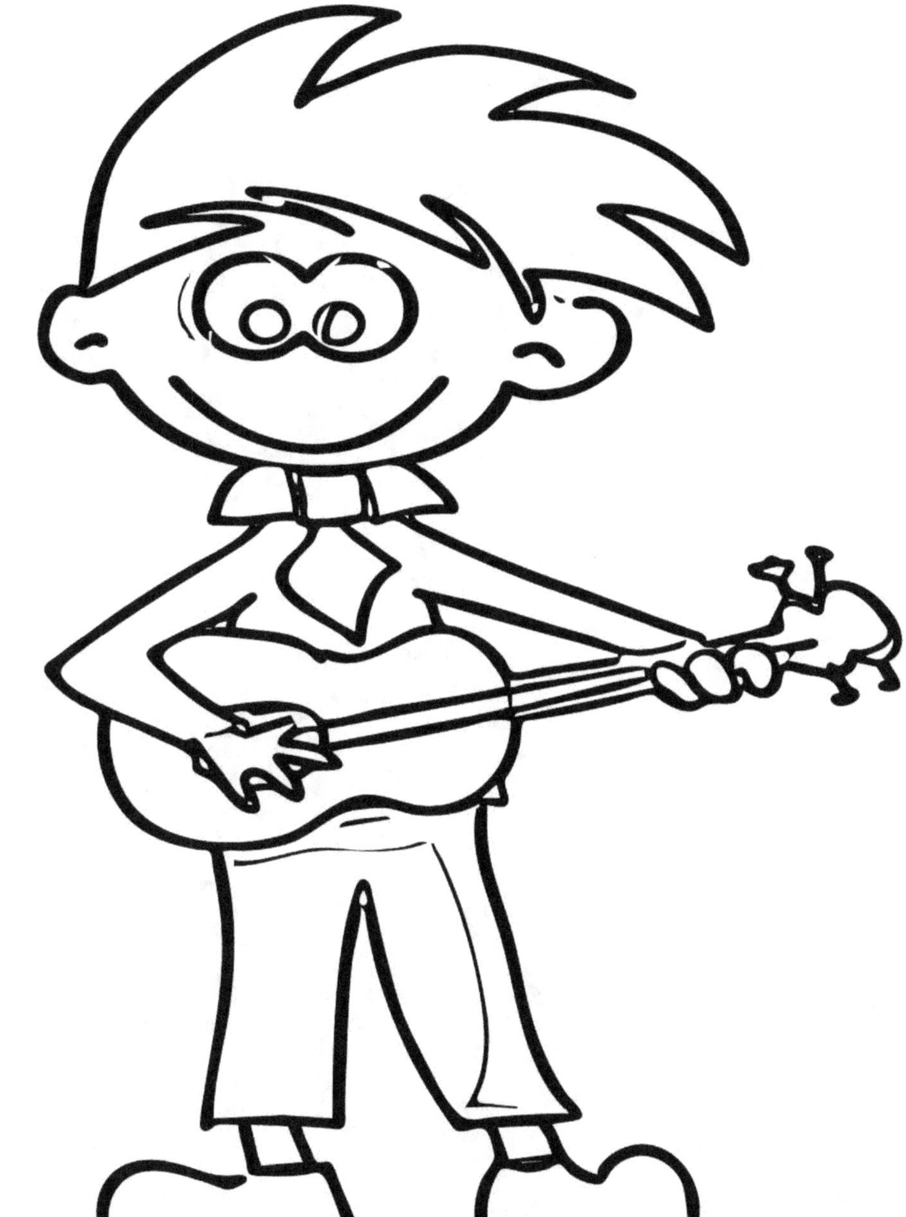

www.ingramcontent.com/pod-product-compliance
Lightning Source LLC
Chambersburg PA
CBHW081619170526
45166CB00009B/3033
* 9 7 8 1 5 1 9 2 9 7 6 5 5 *